My Tongue Is Long and Curves

by Joyce Markovics

Consultant:
Christopher Kuhar, PhD
Executive Director
Cleveland Metroparks Zoo
Cleveland, Ohio

BEARPORT
PUBLISHING

New York, New York

Credits

Cover, © Mark Newman/FLPA/Minden Pictures; 4–5, © Lukas Blazek/Dreamstime; 6–7, © blickwinkel/Alamy Stock Photo; 8–9, © Mohana–AntonMeryl/iStock; 10–11, © Judy Whitton/Shutterstock; 12–13, © MarclSchauer/Shutterstock; 14–15, © blickwinkel/Alamy Stock Photo; 16–17, © Lukas Blazek/Dreamstime; 18–19, © Aflo/Corbis; 20–21, © Aflo/Corbis; 22, © dpa picture alliance/Alamy Stock Photo; 23, © Eric Isselee/Shutterstock; 24, © GlobalP/iStock.

Publisher: Kenn Goin
Senior Editor: Joyce Tavolacci
Creative Director: Spencer Brinker
Design: Debrah Kaiser

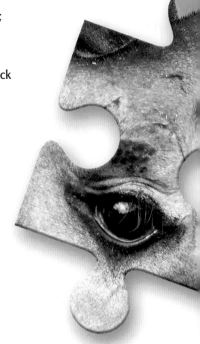

Library of Congress Cataloging-in-Publication Data

Names: Markovics, Joyce L., author.
Title: My tongue is long and curves / by Joyce Markovics.
Description: New York, New York : Bearport Publishing, [2017] | Series: Zoo
  clues 2 | Audience: Ages 6–9._ | Includes bibliographical references and
  index.
Identifiers: LCCN 2016006803 (print) | LCCN 2016009510 (ebook) | ISBN
  9781944102593 (library binding) | ISBN 9781944102593 (ebook)
Subjects: LCSH: Okapi—Juvenile literature.
Classification: LCC QL737.U56 M374 2017 (print) | LCC QL737.U56 (ebook) | DDC
  599.638—dc23
LC record available at http://lccn.loc.gov/2016006803

For more information, write to Bearport Publishing Company, Inc., 45 West 21st Street, Suite 3B, New York, New York 10010. Printed in the United States of America.

10 9 8 7 6 5 4 3 2 1

Contents

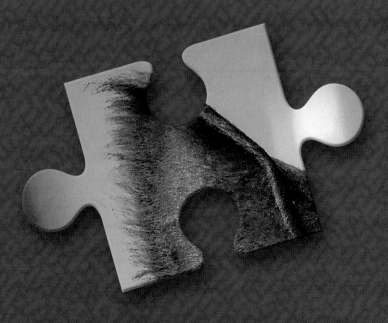

What Am I?

Look at my
ears.

They are large
and furry.

5

6

My legs are slim
and striped.

7

I have big,
oval eyes.

8

9

I have four black hooves.

11

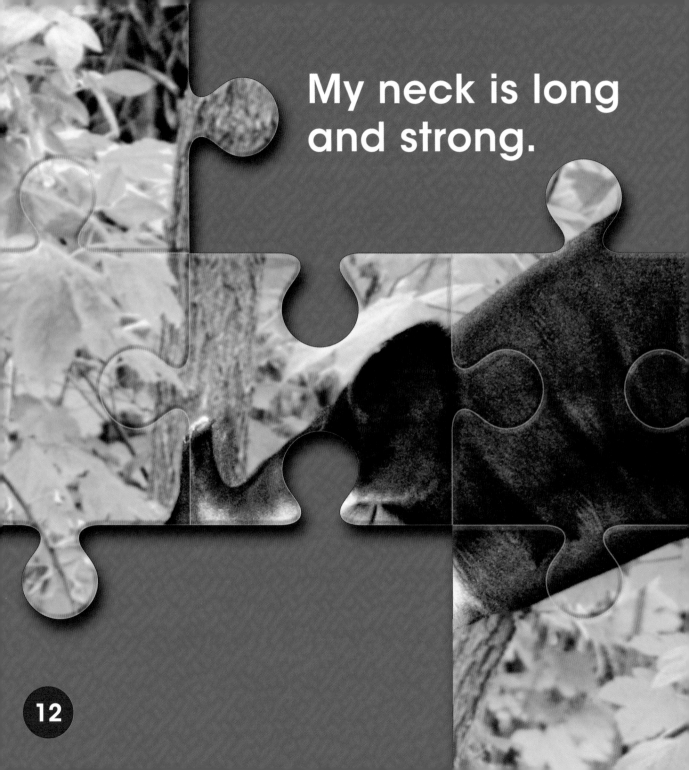

My neck is long and strong.

12

13

I have black, white, and brown fur.

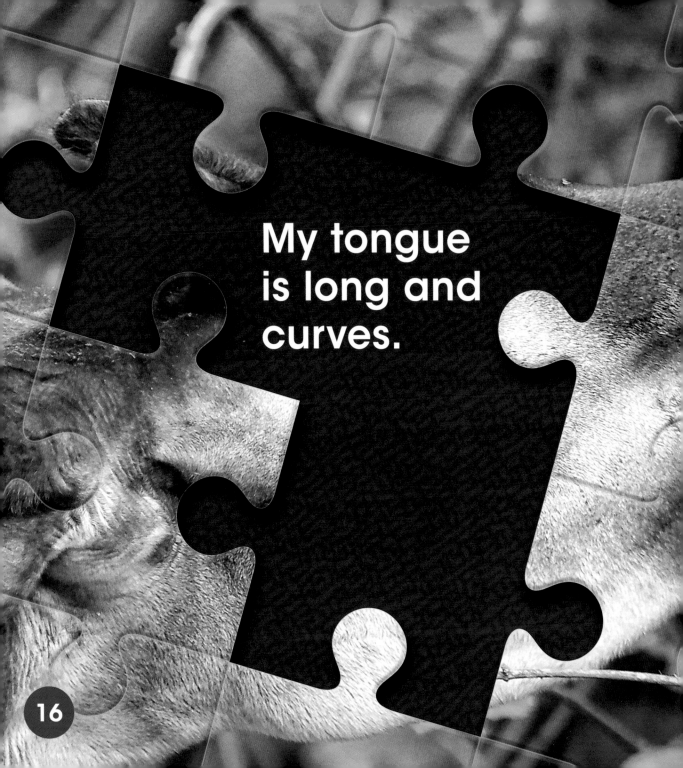

My tongue
is long and
curves.

What am I?

Let's find out!

I am an okapi!

Animal Facts

Okapis (oh-COP-eez) are not zebras or horses. In fact, they are related to giraffes! Like almost all mammals, okapis give birth to live young that drink milk.

More Okapi Facts

Food:	Leaves, twigs, and fruit
Size:	4 to 6.5 feet (1.2 to 2 m) tall at the shoulder
Weight:	400 to 800 pounds (181 to 363 kg)
Life Span:	20 to 30 years
Cool Fact:	An okapi's tongue is so long that the animal can lick its own ears!

Adult Okapi Size

Where Do I Live?

Okapis live in thick, wet forests in Africa.

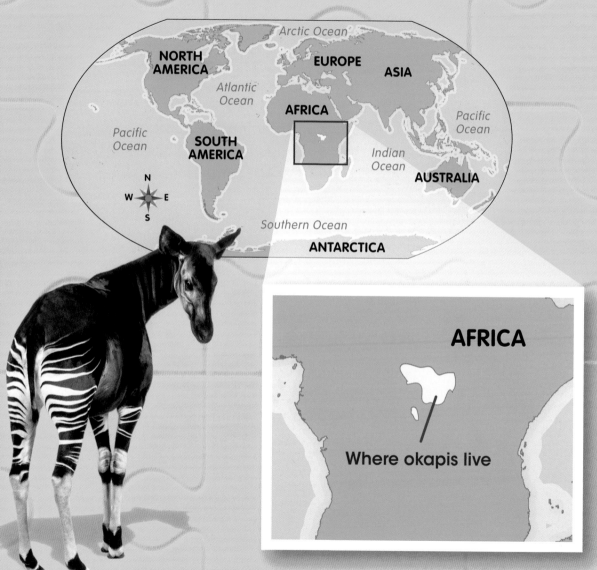

Where okapis live

Index

Read More

Antill, Sarah. *Okapi (Unusual Animals).* New York: Windmill Books (2010).

Galko, Francine. *Rain Forest Animals (Animals in Their Habitats).* Minneapolis, MN: Heinemann (2002).

Learn More Online

To learn more about okapis, visit
www.bearportpublishing.com/ZooClues

About the Author

Joyce Markovics lives in a very old house in Ossining, New York. She enjoys spending time with furry, finned, and feathered creatures.